God Bless America!
Patriotic Poems for Our Times

God Bless America!
Patriotic Poems for Our Times

Adib R. Mikhail, M.D.

For Information, write:

Kingsley Literary Services
6065 Hillcroft, Suite 525
Houston, TX 77081

ISBN 1-931823-15-4

Designed and printed by

Kingsley Literary Services, Ltd
Houston, Texas

www.bookdesigns.net
bookdesigns@halcyon-press.com

This book is dedicated to my son,

Alan Mark Mikhail

. . . who inspires me,

. . . challenges me to write,

. . . and criticizes my writing.

Contents 🦉

Acknowledgments 🦅

Quesna is a small village in the Monofia province in Egypt's Nile delta. In the late 1940's, I was a seven year-old playing during lazy summer months on the grounds of the girl's school my father owned. My friends and I discovered hundreds of strange looking bags hidden in the classrooms. Though they appeared to be the size of a bed pillow, I could see that each was heavy enough that it could barely be carried by a man. I could make out words in English but their meaning was unclear to me. Each bag was stamped: "Gift of the United States Government." We climbed on the bags as though they were stair steps and kept jumping up and down until the groundskeeper Toma admonished us. "These are gifts from America. You cannot play on those bags or I will report you to your father."

This was a rare ultimatum from Toma. It made me wonder what the bags were for, so I asked him. He said, "These bags are flour sent from America. You are asking too many questions. It doesn't matter where America is. What matters is that Americans are good people who try to help our people here."

At dinner that evening, I told my dad about my big discovery. He became serious and said, "These bags from America are not to play on. We are one of the distribution centers in town. Soon we are going to distribute this food to all the hungry people in our area."

"Where is America?" I asked. "Is it near England?" That was the only foreign country I had heard of at that young age.

"It's much farther away. We have one big sea and one big ocean between us," he said.

"So, why are they sending these bags of food to the people of Egypt?"

My father said, "Good people help people in need even when they don't know them and even when they are far, far away. And good people don't expect anything in return. Americans are good people and America is a good country."

That was my first connection with America and it was a most powerful connection!

From that early time I was in awe of America. That's why I acknowledge America and the American people for their generosity which is the inspiration for the poems in this book.

* * *

I especially thank Michelle Sierpina; without her I would not continue to write poems. She encouraged me to write poems even after I stopped writing after the first two poems. Without her advice this book would not be possible or even imaginable.

I also thank my parents, who admired America from afar and taught me to ask questions, learn new things, remain open-minded, and believe in education all throughout life.

Adib R. Mikhail, M.D.
August 2003
The Woodlands, Texas

America . . .

. . . how magical you are

... how magical you are . . .

America . . .

The Story behind "America"

I grew up in Egypt admiring the Founding Fathers of the American Revolution. Though I am a native Egyptian whose first language is Arabic, those American heroes were magical to me. I admired the authors of the Declaration of Independence, especially Thomas Jefferson. I always wanted to visit his home, but I was unable to do so until October 8, 1991. At that time, I went to Washington, D.C., for the fall meeting of the Republican Presidential Roundtable. I invited a friend to attend the meeting on the condition that we would also visit Monticello.

After a two-hour drive from Washington, we arrived at Monticello. When we entered Jefferson's house, the passion for America from my childhood swept over me. I broke down, overwhelmed with tears. My friend could not believe it. I was surprised myself. I went to the hotel, attended the reception, and heard a patriotic speech. I stayed up late. Before I went to bed, I looked out the window and saw the lighted Lincoln Memorial. It was a sight to be seen.

I awakened at 4 o'clock in the morning sobbing with the emotion of the previous evening. I was overcome by an intense desire to write about my feelings. I grabbed the hotel stationery — the only paper handy — and wrote down this poem in English.

It was the first poem I had ever written in any language.

America 🦅

Did you ever really know...
> *... how much I love you?*
> *... how beautiful you are?*
> *... how graceful you are?*
> *... how much I expect from you?*

Did you ever really know...
> *... you are God's country?*
> *... how the world looks up to you?*
> *... how much the world expects from you?*
> *... how magical you are to immigrants?*

Did you ever really know...
> *... that there are no limits to what you can do?*
> *... that the best is yet to come?*
> *... that you have inspired Jefferson, Washington, and Lincoln?*
> *... that you are the best, last hope for humanity?*

Did you ever really know...
> *... that you are going through a mid-life crisis?*
> *... that you can do anything you want?*
> *... that you don't need guns, drugs, or crime?*
> *... how much I care?*

Did you ever really know how beautiful you are?
Did you ever really know how much I love you?

I wish you could!

God Bless America

The Story behind "When You Say America"

In March 2001 an American Air Force reconnaissance plane was escorted by the Chinese Air Force and forced to land on Chinese soil. I watched international news reports regularly to see when and how this incident would end. One of the Chinese propagandists said, "When you say America, you will think of spying." My blood began to boil! I wrote the poem, "When You Say America" in answer to his comment.

When You Say America

When you say America,
You are talking about the guardian of freedom.

When you say America,
You are talking about the protector of human rights.

When you attack America,
You attack life, liberty, and the pursuit of happiness.

When you attack America,
You attack the Superpower of Morality.

When you say America,
You are talking about the protector of minorities.

When you say America,
You are talking about the guardian of the persecuted.

When you say America
You are talking about the nation of nations
and the hope of the world.

The Story behind "When You Say The Bushes"

At the same time that I wrote "When You Say America," I wrote, "When You Say the Bushes" to show my longstanding admiration for the Bush family. I first met Mrs. Bush with her husband in 1978 when he had just retired as Chief of the CIA. They were dressed in shorts watching a national tennis doubles match at The Woodlands outside Houston, Texas. How humble. How decent. He said the three things in life that are the most important are faith, family, and friends. They live with that motto to this day.

When You Say The Bushes

When you say the Bushes,
You are talking about integrity.

When you say the Bushes,
You are talking about morality.

When you say the Bushes,
You are talking about family values.

When you say the Bushes,
You are talking about faith.

When you say the Bushes,
You are talking about friends.

When you attack the Bushes,
You attack the best in America.

When you attack the Bushes,
You attack the conscience of America.

When you attack the Bushes,
You attack American values.

God bless The Bushes!

President and Mrs. George H.W. Bush

The Story behind "Did You Ever Know"

In the summer of 1991, the politics of the U. S. Presidential campaign had begun. I was surprised by the attacks against President George H. W. Bush. I saw him as a great President, who just won the most compelling, quick military victory in American history. Such a great victory had not occurred since the Second World War in 1945. I was particularly upset and irritated by Senator Tom Harkin of Iowa, who was running for President as a Democrat. He started each of his campaign speeches by saying, "To George Herbert Walker Bush..."

I was angry at his way of addressing the President of the United States. I thought he was rude and insulting. I had no way of answering the Senator. I had never written a poem, in any language, before that day in October 1991 when I was attending the fall meeting of the Republican Presidential Roudtable in Washington. I awakened early in the morning after the first meeting and wrote a poem in tribute to America. Unable to return to sleep, half an hour later, I wrote the second poem that I had ever written entitled, "To George Herbert Walker Bush." It was written as a response to the words of Senator Harkin. After writing it, I was relieved, relaxed, and wanted to return to sleep.

Putting those thoughts down on paper allowed me to return to a restful night's sleep.

Did You Ever Know?

For George Herbert Walker Bush

Did you ever know...
>   *...how much you are loved?*
>   *...how much is expected of you?*
>   *...how much more we dare of you?*
>   *...how much more you can do?*

Did you ever know...
>   *...what you have done for democracy?*
>   *...what you have done for peace?*
>   *...what you have done for America?*
>   *...what you have done for Americans?*

I have seen you in Prague, and in a school with a young boy.

Did you ever know...
>   *...how grateful people are to you?*
>   *...how high you help people to dream?*
>   *...how many babies are named for you?*
>   *...how much you have done for believers, for non-believers?*

Did you ever know...
>   *...how genuine you are?*
>   *...you are inspired by the Maestro of the world?*
>   *...how much you are loved?*

I wish you knew!

The Story behind "God Bless Mrs. Barbara Bush"

I admire the Bushes, especially their relationship with their children. One seldom sees any children anywhere in the world who admire their parents more. During the Presidential election campaign of 2000, I observed Mrs. Barbara Bush. I admired her self-control in spite of political attacks on her eldest son. I watched her during the process of recounting the votes after the election. Again, I watched her during the inauguration and afterward. She had become the first First Lady ever to see her son sworn in as President of the United States. (Abigail Adams died before her son John Quincy Adams was elected.)

How proud Mrs. Bush must have been. How proud she must be. She is the Queen Mother of our nation. She inspired my poem, "God Bless Mrs. Barbara Bush."

God Bless Mrs. Barbara Bush 🦅

God has blessed Mrs. Barbara Bush abundantly!

He blessed her with...

> ...a great husband
> ...a great family
> ...great friends

He blessed her to be the first First Lady to see...

> ...her son sworn in as President of the USA

She must be an extraordinary person...

> ...and she is!

She must be an immensely kind person...

> ...and she is!

She must be a caring person...

> ...and she is!

She must be a very generous person...

> ...and she is!

God bless Mrs. Barbara Bush!

In my opinion, the Declaration of Independence and Constitution of the United States of America are the most sacred documents ever written by humankind.

In my opinion, the Declaration of Independence and Constitution of the United States of America are the most sacred documents ever written by humankind.

The Story behind "To Those Who Attack America"

The 9/11 attack left me numb for many days. There were so many floods of emotions I could not begin to sort them out. America's values were seen in contrast to other values. The country's reaction to 9/11 was awe-inspiring. It showed how this country loves to build, to invent, and to prosper while some other cultures hate, destroy, and kill. I wrote the poem to send a message to those others about what America really means.

To Those Who Attack America 🦅

When you attack America,
You attack the Guardian of Freedom.

When you attack America,
You attack the protector of human rights.

When you attack America,
You attack the Mother of all Revolutions.

When you attack America,
You attack the Land of the Free and the Home of the Brave.

When you attack America,
You will always be a loser.

If you don't believe me, ask Tojo of Japan or
Hitler of Germany.
Bin Laden's time will definitely come.

How badly they are mistaken about America's will.

How badly they are mistaken about America!

The Story behind "Ground Hero"

I watched a lot of television after the 9/11 attack. Everybody was talking about Ground Zero. The area meant more to me than those words expressed. At the memorial ceremony for the 9/11 victims at St. Patrick Cathedral in New York, I found my answer. It was then that the Archbishop of New York said, "Nobody should say Ground Zero, everybody should say Ground Hero because this is the place where our heroes are buried."

I held those words in my heart. The poem "Ground Hero" came from that place.

Ground Hero 🦅

They called it Ground Zero.

But it contained so many heroes,
It should be called "Ground Hero"

What is it?

It is 16 acres in the middle of New York.
Ten hateful men destroyed the Twin Towers.

The largest two buildings in the largest city
In the greatest country in the world!

Ten hateful men have destroyed six buildings.
The largest destruction ever known in peace time.

What is it?

It is the area where fire was active for three months.
It is an area of land representing a bleeding wound in the world.

Ground Hero is an attack on the world civilization.

Ground Hero is an attack on the world religions.

Ground Hero is a reminder of what Americans are.

Ground Hero shows what hate can do.

Ground Hero shows how heroes are made.

The Story behind "The Statue of Liberty is Still There"

On September 10, 2001, I returned to Houston after two weeks in New York City where I had attended the U. S. Open Tennis Tournament. My hotel room in New York looked at the two tallest buildings in the World Trade Center. Each night before retiring, I gazed at those buildings.

On September 11, 2001, at 7:50 a.m. Houston time, I was watching television. Suddenly, I noticed one of those very buildings on fire on the screen. I imagined a small airplane might have hit it accidentally. Then the second airplane hit. In astonishment, I realized that the U. S. was under attack.

I phoned my son in California to awaken him with the news. I became numb. I didn't leave the house. For two days I remained fixated on the television trying to make sense of what happened…trying to understand. A flood of emotions came over me and remained for many days.

In 1968, I left Egypt trying to escape religious persecution. The official religion of that country is Islam and I am a Christian. Now, 33 years later, radical Moslem terrorists had come to my new homeland, God's Promised Land. Later in September, a distraught television reporter was surveying the damage in New York City and said, "Everything is gone. I don't know if even the Statue of Liberty is still standing."

In October, I wrote this poem in response to his comment.

The Statue of Liberty is Still There

They stole four planes
they cannot make.
They destroyed two buildings
they cannot build.
But, they can never attack
America's soul…
They can never attack the
Statue of Liberty.

They can destroy airplanes.
They can destroy buildings.
But, they will never be able to
destroy America's values.
The Statue of Liberty is
still there.

They can destroy things.
They can kill innocent people.
But, they will never destroy
America's spirit.
The Statue of Liberty will
always be there!

The Story behind "What 9/11 Means to America"

Recently when I visited the Middle East, some pro-American friends asked me if America is becoming too aggressive against Muslim countries. "Is America determined to destroy Islam?" they asked me.

In response, I explained that they have to remember the great tragedy of 9/11 – the greatest disaster ever. They were not as aware of its effects as they should have been.

At the same time, other friends said, "You know, America was also too wide open to anybody who wanted to enter. There were no security checks." I wrote this poem in an attempt to explain to all America's friends everywhere – and there are many – how 9/11 changed our country forevermore.

What 9/11 Means to America 🦅

9/11

It was the greatest manmade disaster during peacetime in all of history.

It happened during daylight in the world's most media observed country.

It was seen live while it was occurring.

It had a great effect…it shattered America's long-standing false security.

9/11

It brought America to the level of others who had been attacked before.

It shattered psychological barriers for terrorists.

It forced this generous, open country to question its generosity.

It made this country of immigrants question some of its newcomers.

9/11

It forced this fair country to suspect some of its own citizens.

The terrorists must never be forgiven for what they did to this great country!

God Bless America!